背著
Carrying

Gwenyth S

Chinese translation by David Tsai

MILET

LONDON

For my father, G. Henry Swain, who used to carry me on his shoulders

To find out more about the pictures in this book, turn to page 22.
To find out more about sharing this book with children, turn to page 24.

The photographs in this book are reproduced through the courtesy of: ELCA photo library. Used by permission of Augsburg Fortress, front cover, p. 20; © John Elk III, back cover, p. 21; © Elaine Little/World Photo Images, pp. 1, 4; © Lyn Hancock, p. 3; Red Sea Mission Team, Inc., p. 5; © Gerald Cubitt, p. 6; Aramco World Magazine, p. 7; © Trip/M Jelliffe, pp. 8, 16; Heinz Kluetmeier/Dot Photos, p. 9; Piotr Kostrzewski/Cross Cultural Adventures, p. 10; World Bank Photo, p. 11; Jim Hubbard, p. 12; © Lyn Hancock, p. 13; Laurie Nelson, p. 14; Agency for International Development, p. 15; Hans Olaf Pfannkuch, p. 17; Photo Action USA, Cy White, p. 18; Ray Witlin; World Bank Photo, p. 19.

Carrying/Small World Series

Milet Limited
Publishing & Distribution
PO Box 9916, London W14 0GS, England
Email: orders@milet.com
Web site: www.milet.com

First English–Chinese dual language edition published by Milet Limited in 2000
First English edition published in 1999 by Carolrhoda Books, Inc., USA

Copyright © Carolrhoda Books, Inc., 1999
Copyright © Milet Limited for English-Chinese edition, 2000

ISBN 1 84059 124 2

Typeset by Typesetters Ltd, Hertford, England
Printed and bound in the United States of America

你背著什麼呢？
What do you carry?

在上學的路上，你背了書嗎？

Do you carry your books on the way to school?

當你需要讓自己保持涼快時，
你會提著你的鞋子嗎？
Do you carry your shoes
when you need to stay cool?

我們背的東西有可能很大

The things we carry can be very large

或很小。
or very small.

在秋天，我們為了生火背了柴枝
We carry sticks for a fire

和變色的葉子。
and coloured leaves in fall.

有人；有時候；會背著你走一段路嗎？
Does someone, sometimes,
carry you?

關心我們的人，常常會背著我們走一段路！

Often, the people who care for us, carry us, too!

一個有孩子的媽媽要付出很大的代價。

A mother with babies
has much to hold.

但是，當她老的時候，她也需要她小孩的扶助。
But she'll have help from her children
when she grows old.

背是分享負擔，
Carrying means sharing a load,

把食物拿到桌上，或往路的一頭前進。
bringing food to the table,
or moving down the road.

當你為別人背東西時，
When you carry things for others,

你伸出了援手。
you lend a helping hand.

背提高了精神

Carrying lifts the spirit

而且使我們強壯。
and makes us strong.

它讓一段長路變短了。

It makes a long road short.

它告訴了我們，我們有歸屬。

It tells us we belong.

More about the Pictures

Front cover: In Cameroon, a country in West Africa, two girls carry babies—one real and one a doll.

Back cover: A young boy at a monastery in India holds a key.

Page 1: A boy carries fish to the market on Jolo, an island in the Philippines.

Page 3: An Inuit girl carries her doll on her back in Nunavut, a territory in northern Canada.

Page 4: In the Philippines, a boy brings his books home from school.

Page 5: A girl carries her shoes and a bucket on a hot day in Mali, a West African country.

Page 6: Girls balance jars full of well water on their heads in Rajasthan in northwestern India.

Page 7: In the desert of Algeria, a country in North Africa, a boy holds a stick toy.

Page 8: A girl in Cameroon brings home wood for the fire.

Page 9: A boy in Russia takes a fallen leaf as his prize.

Page 10: A woman in Mali carefully carries her two babies.

 **Page 11:** In South Korea, an older woman cares for—and carries—a small child.

 **Page 12:** Twins are a heavy load for this mother in Washington, D.C.

 **Page 13:** An Inuit woman and her daughter carry children on their backs in Nunavut, Canada.

 **Page 14:** In Peru, men work together to carry a symbol of the Virgin Mary during Candelaria, a festival.

 **Page 15:** In Nepal, a girl climbs a steep road while carrying a child.

 **Page 16:** A girl in Cameroon sells *mandasi* (cooked dough balls).

 **Page 17:** In Senegal, a country in West Africa, two boys work together to get water from a well.

 **Page 18:** In Milwaukee, Wisconsin, a clown lifts a little girl above the crowd, lifting her spirits, as well.

 **Page 19:** A woman in Ethiopia balances a heavy water-filled gourd on her head.

 **Page 20:** Two young women make a journey together in Cameroon.

 **Page 21:** Boy Scouts in Bangkok, Thailand, take part in a water-carrying contest.

A Note to Adults on Sharing This Book

Help your child become a lifelong reader. Read this book together, taking turns as you both read out loud. Look over the photographs and choose your favourites. Sound out new words and come back to them later for review. Then try these "extensions"—activities that extend the experience of reading and build discussion and problem-solving skills.

Talk about Carrying

All around the world, you can find people carrying things—and other people. Discuss with your child the things people carry. How do the people shown in this book carry things? How does your child carry things to school? How do ways of carrying things or people differ? How are they the same?

Carry Things in Different Ways

With your child, gather a few unbreakable objects you can carry, such as a book, a brush, or a rucksack. Try carrying each object in three different ways: on or over your shoulder, on your head, and in your hand. Which way of carrying each thing seemed easier or harder? Ask your child why certain objects were easier to carry one way than another.